Y0-AWH-737

CANADA

Tracy Vonder Brink

TABLE OF CONTENTS

Canada...3

Glossary... 22

Index... 24

A Crabtree Seedlings Book

CRABTREE
Publishing Company
www.crabtreebooks.com

School-to-Home Support for Caregivers and Teachers

This book helps children grow by letting them practice reading. Here are a few guiding questions to help the reader with building his or her comprehension skills. Possible answers appear here in red.

Before Reading:

• What do I think this book is about?
  • *I think this book is about Canada.*
  • *I think this book is about the people of Canada.*

• What do I want to learn about this topic?
  • *I want to learn about the animals that live in Canada.*
  • *I want to learn about the cities in Canada.*

During Reading:

• I wonder why...
  • *I wonder why Canada and the United States share Niagara Falls.*
  • *I wonder why more than 7,000 black bears live on Vancouver Island.*

• What have I learned so far?
  • *I have learned that the northern lights are colored lights that sometimes glow in the night sky in Northern Canada.*
  • *I have learned that Toronto is the biggest city in Canada.*

After Reading:

• What details did I learn about this topic?
  • *I have learned that Ottawa is the capital of Canada.*
  • *I have learned that Québec is more than 400 years old.*

• Read the book again and look for the vocabulary words.
  • *I see the word **canal** on page 4, and the word **migrate** on page 20. The other glossary words are found on pages 22 and 23.*

Canada is a country.

It is in **North America**.

CANADA

OTTAWA

Ottawa is Canada's **capital**.

A **canal** flows through it.

The water freezes in winter.

People enjoy skating on the ice.

Most people in Canada speak English. Some also speak French. **Indigenous** peoples also have their own languages.

5

Niagara Falls is in the South, along the Niagara River.

Niagara Falls has three waterfalls.

Niagara Falls flows between Canada and the United States. The two countries share it.

Toronto is also in the South.

It is Canada's largest city by population, or the number of people who live there.

Toronto has tall buildings.

The CN Tower is one of the tallest in the world.

Québec is a city in the East.

It is more than 400 years old.

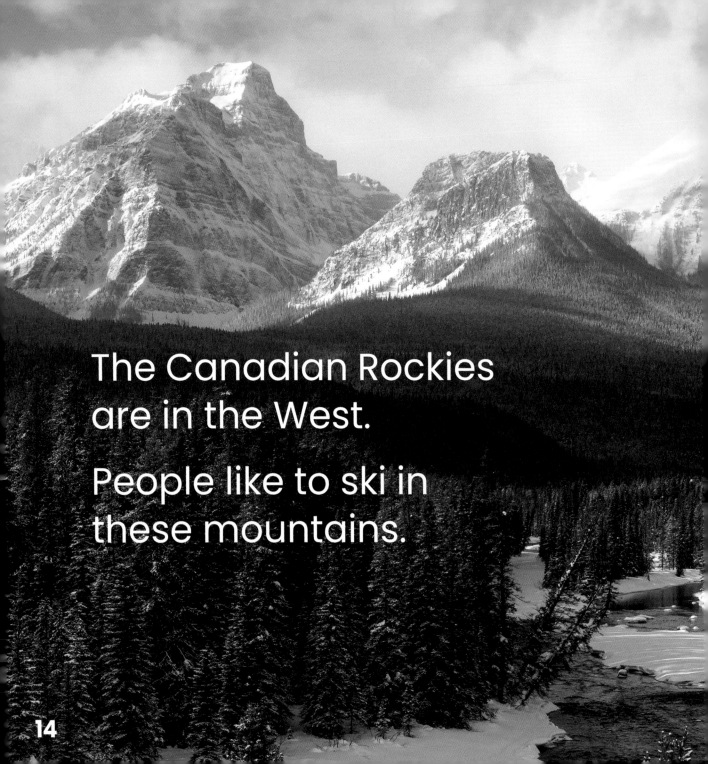

The Canadian Rockies are in the West.

People like to ski in these mountains.

Vancouver Island is also in the West.

More than 7,000 black bears live there.

Whales swim near the **coast**.

Northern Canada is very cold in winter.

The **northern lights** glow in the night sky.

The energy that makes the northern lights comes from the Sun.

Polar bears live in the North.

Every year they **migrate** between the land and the ice.

Canada has big cities and wild nature!

Glossary

canal (kuh-NAL): A human-made waterway used to get boats from place to place or to bring water to farmland

capital (KAP-i-tl): The city where the government of a country or a state is located

coast (kohst): The land next to the ocean or sea

Indigenous (in-DIJ-uh-nuhs): The first people to live in an area. In Canada, Indigenous peoples are First Nations, Inuit, and Métis.

North America (NORth uh-MEH-rih-kuh): One of Earth's seven continents

northern lights (NOR-thrn lites): Large areas of colored light that sometimes appear in the night sky in the Far North

migrate (MY-grayt): To move from one area to another when the season changes

Index

Niagara Falls 6, 7

northern lights 18, 19

Ottawa 4

polar bears 20

Toronto 8, 10

Vancouver Island 16

About the Author

Tracy Vonder Brink

Tracy Vonder Brink loves to visit new places. She has been to Niagara Falls and watched the beautiful waterfalls. She lives in Cincinnati with her husband, two daughters, and two rescue dogs.

CRABTREE
Publishing Company

Written by: Tracy Vonder Brink
Designed by: Under the Oaks Media
Proofreader: Janine Deschenes
Production coordinator
   and Prepress technician: Tammy McGarr
Print coordinator: Katherine Berti

Photographs:
Shutterstock: Maurizio De Mattei: cover; Hanna Mariay: p. 3; Agnus Febriyant: p. 5; Colin Temple: p. 5(b); ArKXp: 6-7; Kiev.Victo: p. 9; Diego Grandi: p. 11; R.M. Nunes: p. 13; EBAdventures Photography: p. 14-15; Top Mark Vount: p. 17 (top); jaredblankscott: p. 17 (bottom); Ken Phung: p. 19; miroslav chytil: p. 21

Library and Archives Canada Cataloguing in Publication
CIP available at Library and Archives Canada

Library of Congress Cataloging-in-Publication Data
CIP available at Library of Congress

Crabtree Publishing Company

www.crabtreebooks.com   1-800-387-7650

Printed in the U.S.A./CG20210915/012022

Published in the United States
Crabtree Publishing
347 Fifth Avenue, Suite 1402-145
New York, NY, 10016

Published in Canada
Crabtree Publishing
616 Welland Ave.
St. Catharines, ON, L2M 5V6